Life's Symphony of Love and Heartbreak

By Lunar Patni

This book is dedicated to the memory of Erik

Erik, I'll see you on the other side,
my love

PART ONE

Firework

I see you across the table and a
million fireworks explode in my heart
Your pride burns gold
Our nonexistent love favors bright and
dark red sparks, sparks unlike ours
The romance I wish to obtain with you
shines rose
I like you
I like you so much
But you don't even exist
You're just an idea
I wish you were a real person

I wish I could fall in love too

At least I don't have to get
heartbroken now

Planets

I crave to ask Saturn how she gained
so many suitors, all willing to give
her rings

I yearn to ask Pluto if they are okay,
and how the loneliness feels, even
though I already know

I thirst to ask Venus how it feels to
be the planet of love, but unable to
find love for themself

I hunger to ask Mars about the anger
he feels, maybe I could help him

I dream of telling a black hole,
"You're not as alone as you think"

I lost faith in the world when I was nine.

If you called in the middle of the
night I'd still answer

I can

I can stand alone
I can live alone
I can stand strong
I can live long
And I'll still be better than you
You know it.

But I don't want
to have
to be alone

On a bad day, a blanket can weigh a
thousand pounds

I want the love I give.

Is that selfish?

I hope a boy my age finds these books

I hope he smiles

I hope he falls in love with me and my words

Instead of me, despite my words

You're the coldest water I've ever
been baptized in

When you don't speak, you learn to listen

When you listen, you hear everything

My love is an overfilled cup
Too much, so no one wants it

Juiced and Drained

I've been juiced of all my ideas
All my creativity
I have nothing left to give
Nothing more to be good for
And yet I still write
Because that is what I was meant to do
So I will write
And write
And write
And one day it will all be worth it
Even if I'm currently drained of ideas

PART TWO

Poems for Her.

Every angel in Heaven knows your name,
your title

Every day I ask them why they're down
on earth and not up with the others

I feel more alone with you than without

Cherry Blossom Girl

Oh beautiful cherry blossom girl
I love your petals, pink and rosy
I love your branches, thin and wiry
I love your trunk, steady and reliable
I love your roots, loyal and strong

Oh beautiful cherry blossom girl
You dress like a hippie but I'd call you a psychic
You can see right through me

Please find pity in that gorgeous
heart of yours for a lowlife like me

I love you is the most expensive phrase.

It always costs something

Sunshine

Your smile is the sunshine of the world
I'd give you anything you ask to see that gorgeous smile
Take my heart, take my soul, take the stars, just show me a ray of light, my love
I'd give you the world
Just to call you mine

You may be out of my league

But you're never out of my head

Lend me your heart and I'll show you the stars

Your beauty intimidates me the way a thousand bears would

I know you're speaking but all I can
hear is church bells

You're only mine in my dreams

But oh, what wonderful dreams they are

She smiles and the world goes silent

I'd steal the stars for you

She knows.

She knows.
Of course, she knows.
I wasn't subtle enough I guess
She knows and I'm dead because she doesn't care
The voice of a siren, the face of a goddess, I'm not surprised
I knew she wouldn't feel the same
She's perfect
And I'm just me

Let me kiss the ground you walk on,
for every footstep of yours is a
treasure

I'm homesick for you

You are the poem I can't find the
words to write

Sharing a drink with you is the
equivalent of drinking a golden
ambrosia made of the sunsets

You are a rose in a garden of withered
weeds

My heart has traveled millions of
miles to find you

Die for you

I would die for you, yes
But I'd also live for you
I'd stop cutting for you
I'd study for you
I'd get out of bed for you
I'd break my heart for you
I'd never read again for you
I starve for you
I'd kill for you

My eyes are open

And yet I dream of only you

You're my celebrity crush

Deserve

Let me treat you the way you deserve, love
Let me massage you after a long day
Let me brush my fingers through your hair
Let me run you a bath
I'll do anything you ask, my love, and even the things you don't ask for and just want
Let me treat you the way you deserve

Heads turn when you walk past people
in the halls

I want to rip their eyes out
They don't deserve you.
They're not good enough for you

PART THREE

POEMS FOR NATHAN

The lonely boy I wish to hold

The day death takes my hand I will cry
Not because I have lost my life
But because I'm holding someone's hand
And that someone isn't you

If your happiness were a drop of water
my goal would be to flood the desert.

I love you.
I love you so so much.
I love you more than I could ever
love anything or anyone
And yet
You do not even like me

This section of my book has concluded rather abruptly, but that's okay.

That's the way all relationships end

And in the end, that's all my book is,
A sour collection of relationships

Nathan's section of this book also concluded rather quickly, as did his chapter in my life. I hope he's okay

Loverdosed

I've loverdosed for no one in
particular
But I'm gone
I'm passed out never to return again
Only because of the love I've never
been able to have
Or accept.

My love turns me into a mother with a stillborn child
My heart is beating for someone who's isn't

I love you, Erik.

PART FOUR
Benjamin

The Sun and the Moon

I am the Sun
You are the Moon
I wait all day for a simple text for
you that I won't receive.
Not because you mean
Not because you don't love me
But because we're miles apart.
There are only a few hours each day
when we can talk and it is torture
But oh, oh my love.
When I talk to you for even a minute
it's all worth it.

I

I chase you like a cat chases a mouse.
The cat wants a friend
The mouse is too scared to be that
friend
So he runs
And so do I, in a neverending cycle

If I let you bite me, will you tell me
what I taste like?

Timeless

Poetry does not already exist, poetry is made.

A flower is just a flower until a poet renames it Demeter's soul.

Trees were just trees before being called Weeping willows

The sun was just the sun before being a great ball of golden light, giving life to those so bright.

Except you.

You've always been like this, haven't you?

You've always been poetry, always been just ink on paper written with a typewriter, or maybe a golden-tipped quill.

You are extraordinary.

timeless.

Sixth sense

"Never forget me"
You whispered to me before you committed.

Like I could forget how to breathe

Like I could forget to feel

Like I could forget to touch

Like I could forget to see

Like I could forget to hear

Like I could forget to taste

As if I could ever forget you in all my lifetimes

I want to plant kisses on your body so my love, our love, can grow. Let me water those seeds with affection and let them bask in sunlight when I take you out. Breathe in my scent and let me nourish your planted kisses until you are a garden full of love.

You are so loved, dear.

"Do you hear that?"

"What?"

"The Gods, begging us to fall in love"

Strip me down and kiss my soul

You are the blank spots in a poem

A place for reflection

A spot of peace and tranquility

Every broken fragment of me loves
every shining mosaic of you

If only I could've met you at the dawn of time

Then I could love you for longer and longer

I want you to know this but I feel
like I shouldn't have to tell you.
Y'know?

The Last Time

You never think that the last time is going to be THE LAST TIME.

YOu always think you have more time

Because they couldn't leave me, right?

Of course not.

We'll have eternity together.

I think it's okay for me to love you

The problem is when I start to think
you love me too

It's almost like I can physically feel
every mile between us

It hurts so much

Does it hurt you too?

Can you feel it?

When I'm with you, I smile like I've never cried

I've known you for a month

I'll mourn you for a year

I'll remember you for a lifetime

How do I greet someone after a year?

You're still unblocked by the way

Just in case

I think you were gone before you left
I could feel it in the way you talked
    Or rather, the way you did

I don't think its hit me yet that
you're gone

Not breakup gone

But dead gone

If I kissed you

Would it convince you to stay?

I'm sick of love

But I'm also so lovesick

I have to write
Because if I don't write
What am I good for?

I don't care if it's not true
Say it again
Even if you do not mean it, I need to
hear those words again
Not for them, but from you
So, please
Please
Say it again

I think-
I think I might like you more than
books
More than romance
More than poetry
More than fall leaves
And maybe even more than warm blankets
Maybe more than candles
And brown sweaters
Maybe even more than music
maybe.

I can't read my old writing
I can't look at old paintings
I can't listen to old songs
They're all about love
When is it not?

I feel like I deserve a high school
sweetheart instead of being a
statistic

Not even a dreamcatcher can keep you
away, love

I don't believe in shooting stars or eyelashes
Fourleaf clovers and pennies in fountains
Candles, feathers, pretty rocks
A lucky pen or jacket or shirt
A card or a number or anything like that
But I want to
I really want to

I'm not watching you
I dont want to
But I know everything you do
sorry

I can't listen to Guitars and drugs
(Sorry John K)
But it was your song, our song
So I can't listen to it anymore

All the solar system and my favorite star

I can't give you the world
But can I write it?

I think I'm addicted to love(ing you)

The night sky is a star's graveyard

I sit on my bed listening to Sailor
Song by Gigi Perez writing sad poetry

And then I smile widely at your stupid
text and blush as we bicker

If you were the ocean I'd confess my
love for you until all of your salt
because sugar and all of your water
became honey

Does falling into you mean I'm over him?

Should I mourn him longer?

Sorry, Erik.

Can I cry you back?

I wave a white flag

But you continue to touch me

What horrible deed did I do to deserve
this body?

The dark hole that is the night sky
and the stars still poke out, wanting,
praying, begging, for just a glimpse
of you.

I think God has finally given in to my
prayers to be loved.
Why else would He have given me you?

You are tangled in my soul like a pair
of headphones.

If you were the sun, I'd watch the
    sunrise every morning

 But I'd also cry every sunset

I think my love for you was sealed
when I talked to you for the first
time and I blinked.

I am a chapter in your life
You are a book,
a full bookshelf overflowing with books,
You are a whole library.

If you love me how I am, then I'll
love you how you are too.

To the Lonely

Go, my poems, to the lonely, to the unwanted
Go to the anxious and be a weapon for their wars, internal and ex.
Go to those thrown to the piles of those broken and helpless and be a chariot for them
Go to the rich, dying of gout
Go to the poor, who wish to be stout
Go to the woman whose crams hurt her soul
Go to the man who wants to give her pure gold
Go be a weapon
Go be the peace
Go be anything my readers desire

Cupid's Crop

Every smile you beam reaps all cupids crops
Cupid cries for I have stolen all his lovely plants and wheat and seeds to feed my love for you

I throw a penny to the fountain
Copper penny
Shiny and cold
And I think
And suddenly I'm running my hands
through your copper penny hair

-wish on a penny

When it is too early to say I love you

But too late to only like you

I don't know what to say

Do you?

He walks, oblivious to how much I love him
His strides are long and slow, and with every step he takes, I somehow love him more
He walks, oblivious to how girls and boys alike swoon when they meet his gaze
He walks, oblivious to anything but the nature and wildlife around him
He walks, and I love him more

Whoever you are
Wherever you are
Whenever you are
   I'll love you

Tell him

Go, my wordy book, and tell him how beautiful he is

Tell him the sunsets do not compare to the fire in his eyes
Or the one in my heart

Tell him that when he speaks, pearls fall out of his mouth like a cracked-open oyster

Tell him a night with him is a night in heaven

Tell him his eyes shine like the stars in Orion's belt when he speaks about something he loves

Speak his name, my dear book, and watch me rise from my grave

Tell him his words are poetry and his voice is music

And tell him his skin is golden and his scars are stunning silver

Tell him I want to kiss every bit of
skin on his body

Tell him I want to kiss him so deep he
feels it in his bones, in his soul

Tell him when I call him annoying and
say I hate him, that all I want to do
is pin him to a wall and let him steal
my first kiss

Tell him... Oh tell him

Tell him how glorious he is to me

Tell him the way he's kept me alive,
kept me sane even

Tell him I love him with the power of
a thousand suns

And tell him it was me who told you to
tell him these things

It's scary, letting my walls down
again
Cause now you won't respond and I'm
alone again
It's really lonely without you
Please come back
Don't leave me
Not like they did

What if I don't want to be a poet anymore?

What if I want to be a poem, a muse?

I don't know how to love nonchalantly

I love obsessively

I love like an overfilled cup or a flooding waterfall

I'm too much though, right?

Who can handle this much love?

Not you

Or maybe you can

Just not from me

111

111 is an angel number

Good fortune, they say

But you left me

New beginnings, they say

But you're the same as them

Opportunity, they say

But you're not here

Greater good, they say

But all I want is you

I write because I can't bring it in me
to pull the trigger

A Lunar Date

Take me to an aquarium
Smile as I squeal and pet the sea
urchins and fish and stingray

I want you to admire my childishness
as I stare at the sharks with a
wonderstruck look on my face

Get me chicken tenders from the cafe
and when I try to pay, slap my hand
away and pull out your wallet. When I
resist, buy me a shake

Take a walk with me in the park and
smile and I pick flowers for you and
wish for you on every dandelion I see

Take me to a rooftop and dance with me
in the rain and laugh when I step on
your feet

Lie down with me off said rooftop and
look over at me when I look at the
stars. Let me lie on your chest and
hold me while we watch a shooting star
and both wish for each other until we
fall asleep.

Wake up in the middle of the night to me shivering and drape your jacket around my shoulders.

www.ingramcontent.com/pod-product-compliance
Lightning Source LLC
LaVergne TN
LVHW092053060526
838201LV00047B/1370